# Dan's Old Van

Written by Kathy Henderson

Illustrated by Andy Hammond

Dan's old van
sang a song as it ran.

# Clang-a-bang-bang! Clang-a-bang-bang!

It went clang-a-bang-bang!
Clang-a-bang-bang!

Its bits didn't fit.
They went slip-slop-slip,

and the rack at the back
went crack-crick-crack,

Crack-crick-crack!

and the box on the top
went rock-rick-rock,

# Click-clack-click!

and the spring on the stick
went click-clack-click.

Pam said, "Stop,
or the bits will drop off!

I can fix it with my kit.
Let me hit it a bit."

*Cling-clang-cling!!*

So she got out some string
and a fixing thing
and went cling-clang-cling,
cling-clang-cling.

Pam said, "That's it.
That will do the trick."

So off went Dan
in his old red van,
and it did not sing
the old clang-a-bang-bing.

No. Not a thing.

It went—

# Bang-a-slip-a-crack-a-rock-a-click-a-clack-a...

bang-a-slip-a-crack-a-rock-a-click-a-clack-a . . .

# PING!